What This Guide Will Do For You

Whether travelling to a foreign country or to your favorite international restaurant, this *Nice & Easy* guide gives you just enough of the language to get around and be understood. Much of the material in this book was developed for government personnel who are often assigned to a foreign country on a moment's notice and need a quick introduction to the language.

In this handy and compact guide, you will find useful words and phrases, popular expressions, common greetings, and the words for numbers, money, and time. Every word or phrase is accompanied with the correct pronunciation and spelling. There is a vocabulary list for finding words quickly.

Generous margins on the pages allow you to make notes and remarks that you may find helpful.

The book begins with a section on Persian history and relevant up-to-date facts on the present country of Iran which should enhance your understanding of the language.

Carl Fuchs
Language Program Director

Contents

PERSIAN
Made Nice & Easy!™

Staff of Research & Education Association
Carl Fuchs, Language Program Director

Based on Language Courses developed by the
U.S. Government for Foreign Service Personnel

Research & Education Association
61 Ethel Road West
Piscataway, New Jersey 08854

Dr. M. Fogiel, Director

PERSIAN MADE NICE & EASY™

Printed in the United States of America

Library of Congress Control Number 2001087399

International Standard Book Number 0-87891-400-5

LANGUAGES MADE NICE & EASY is a trademark of Research & Education Association, Piscataway, New Jersey 08854

IRAN

FACTS & HISTORY

Official Name: Islamic Republic of Iran

Geography
1.6 million sq. km. (636, 294 sq. mi.); slightly larger than Alaska.
Cities: Capital—Tehran. Other cities—Isfahan, Tabriz, Mashhad, Shiraz.
Terrain: Desert and mountains.
Climate: Semiarid; subtropical along the Caspian coast.

People
Nationality: Noun and adjective—Iranian(s).
Population: 61 million. Annual growth rate: 3.5%.
Ethnic groups: Persian; Azeri Turks; Kurds; Arabs; Turkomans and Baluchis; and Lur, Bakhtiari, and Qashqai tribes.
Religions: Shi'ite Muslim 95%; Sunni Muslim 4%; Zoroastrian, Jewish, Christian, and Baha'i 1%.
Languages: Persian, Turkish dialects, Kurdish, Luri, Gilaki, Arabic.
Education: Literacy—50%.

Health: Infant mortality rate—64/1,000. Life expectancy—65 years.
Work force: Agriculture—33%. Manufacturing—21%. There is a shortage of skilled labor.

Government
Type: Islamic republic.
Constitution: Ratified December 1979, revised 1989.
Branches: Executive—"Leader of the Islamic Revolution" (head of state); president and Council of Ministers. Legislative—270-member National Consultative Assembly (Majles). Judicial—Supreme Court.
Political parties: None.
Flag: Three horizontal bands of green, white, and red, with the national emblem, a stylized representation of the word Allah, in the center.

Economy
GDP (est.): $90 billion.
Annual growth rate (est.): 5%.
Per capita income (est.): $1,500.
Natural resources: Petroleum, natural gas, and some mineral deposits.
Agriculture: Principal products—wheat, rice, other grains, sugar beets, fruits, nuts, cotton, dairy products, wool, caviar; not self-sufficient in food.
Industry: Types—petroleum, petrochemicals, textiles, cement and building materials, food processing (particularly sugar refining and vegetable oil produc-

tion), metal fabricating (steel and copper).

Trade: Exports—$18 billion: petroleum 90%, carpets, fruits, nuts, hides. Imports—$28 billion: food, machinery, and medical products.

Major markets/suppliers: Germany, Japan, Italy, U.K., France.

People and Culture

Almost two-thirds of Iran's people are of Aryan origin—their ancestors migrated from Central Asia. The major groups in this category include Persians, Kurds, Lurs, and Baluchi. The remainder are primarily Turkic but also include Arabs, Armenians, Jews, and Assyrians. The 1979 Islamic revolution and the war with Iraq transformed Iran's class structure politically, socially, and economically. In general, however, Iranian society remains divided into urban, market-town, village, and tribal groups. Clerics, called mullahs, dominate politics and nearly all aspects of Iranian life, both urban and rural. After the fall of the Pahlavi regime in 1979, much of the urban upper class of prominent merchants, industrialists, and professionals, favored by the former Shah, lost standing and influence to the senior clergy and their supporters. Bazaar merchants, who were allied with the clergy against the Pahlavi shahs, have also gained political and economic power since the revolution. The urban working class has enjoyed somewhat enhanced status and economic mobility, spurred in part by opportunities provided by revolutionary organizations and the government bureaucracy. Unemployment, a major problem even before the revolution, has many causes, including population growth, the war with Iraq, and shortages of raw materials and trained managers. Farmers and peasants received a psychological boost from the attention given them by the Islamic regime but appear to be hardly better off in economic terms. The government has made progress on rural development, including electrification and road building, but has not yet made a commitment to land redistribution. Most Iranians are Muslims; 95% belong to the Shi'ites branch of Islam, the official state religion, and about 4% belong to the Sunni branch, which predominates in neighboring Muslim countries. Non-Muslim minorities include Zoroastrians, Jews, Baha'is, and Christians.

History of Iran

The ancient nation of Iran, historically known to the West as Persia and once a major empire in its own right, has been overrun frequently and has had its territory altered throughout the centuries. Invaded by Arabs, Seljuk Turks, Mongols, and others—and often caught up in the affairs of larger powers—Iran has always reasserted its national identity and has developed as a distinct political and cultural entity.

Archeological findings have placed knowledge of Iranian prehistory at middle paleolithic times (100,000 years ago). The earliest sedentary cultures date from 18,000-14,000 years ago. The sixth millennium B.C. saw a fairly sophisticated agricultural society and proto-urban population centers. Many dynasties have ruled Iran, the first of which was under the Achaemenians (559-330 B.C.), a dynasty founded by Cyrus the Great. Cyrus led the combined forces of the Medes and the Persians to establish the most extensive empire known in the ancient world. When he died in 529, Cyrus's kingdom extended as far east as the Hindu Kush in present-day Afghanistan. His successors were less successful. The quality of the Achaemenids as rulers began to disintegrate and soon became vulnerable to the plans of Alexander the Great. Envisioning a new world empire based on a fusion of Greek and Persian culture and ideals, Alexander the Great of Macedon accelerated the disintegration of the Achaemenid Empire. In quick succession he took Egypt, Babylonia, and then, over the course of two years, the heart of the Achaemenid Empire. Alexander's reign ended in 323 B.C. when he was struck with fever and died, leaving no heir. After the Hellenistic period (300-250 B.C.) came the Parthian (250 B.C.-226 A.D.) and the Sassanian (226-651) dynasties.

The beduin Arabs who toppled the Sassanid Empire were propelled not only by a desire for conquest but also by a new religion, Islam. The Prophet Muhammad, a member of the Hashimite clan of the powerful tribe of Quraysh, proclaimed his prophetic mission in Arabia in 612 and eventually won over the city of his birth, Mecca, to the new faith. Within one year of Muhammad's death in 632, Arabia itself was secure enough to allow his secular successor, Abu Bakr, the first caliph, to begin the campaign against the Byzantine and Sassanid empires. Abu Bakr defeated the Byzantine army at Damascus in 635 and then began his conquest of Persia.

The seventh-century Arab-Muslim conquest of Iran was followed by conquests by the Seljuk Turks, the Mongols, and Tamerlane. Variously described as of Mongol or Turkic origin, Tamerlane was the next ruler to achieve emperor status. He conquered Transoxiana proper and by 1381 established himself as sovereign. He did not have the huge forces of earlier Mongol leaders, so his conquests were slower and less savage than those of Genghis Khan. Tamerlane's regime was characterized by its inclusion of Persians in administrative roles and its promotion of architecture and poetry. His empire disintegrated rapidly after his death in 1405, however, and Mongol tribes, Uzbeks, and Bayundur Turkomans ruled roughly the area of present-day Iran until the rise of the Safavid dynasty, the first native Iranian dynasty in almost 1,000 years.

Persia underwent a revival under the Safavid dynasty (1502-1736), the most prominent figure of which was Shah Abbas. In addition to his political reorganization with the gradual separation of religious institutions from the state, Shah Abbas also promoted commerce and the arts. The Safavid Empire declined after the death of Shah Abbas. Nader Shah rose to power and drove the Russians from the Iranian coast on the Caspian Sea and restored Iranian sovereignty over Afghanistan. The conqueror Nader Shah and his successors were followed by the Zand dynasty, founded by Karim Kahn, and later the Qajar (1795-1925) and the Pahlavi dynasties (1925-1979).

Modern Iranian history began with a nationalist uprising against the Shah Muzaffar ad Din in 1905, the granting of a limited constitution in 1906, and the discovery of oil in 1908. In 1921, Reza Khan, an Iranian officer of the Persian Cossack Brigade, seized control of the government. In 1925, he made himself Shah, ruling as Reza Shah Pahlavi for almost 16 years and installing the new Pahlavi dynasty. Under his reign, Iran began to modernize and to secularize politics, and the central government reasserted its authority over the tribes and provinces. In September 1941, following the Allies' (U.K.-Soviet Union) occupation of western Iran, Reza Shah was forced to abdicate. His son, Mohammad Reza Pahlavi, became Shah and ruled until 1979. During World War II, Iran was a vital link in the Allied supply line for lend-lease supplies to the Soviet Union. After the war, Soviet troops stationed in northwestern Iran not only refused to withdraw, but backed revolts that established short-lived, pro-Soviet separatist regimes in the northern regions of Azerbaijan and Kurdistan. These were ended in 1946. The Azerbaijan revolt crumbled after U.S. and UN pressure forced a Soviet withdrawal and Iranian forces suppressed the Kurdish revolt.

In 1951, Premier Mohammed Mossadeq, a militant nationalist, forced the parliament to nationalize the British-owned oil industry. Mossadeq was opposed by the Shah and was removed, but he quickly returned to power. The Shah fled Iran but returned when supporters staged a coup against Mossadeq in August 1953. Mossadeq was then arrested by pro-Shah army forces. In 1961, Iran initiated a series of economic, social, and administrative reforms that became known as the Shah's White Revolution. The core of this program was land reform. Modernization and economic growth proceeded at an unprecedented rate, fueled by Iran's vast petroleum reserves, the third-largest in the world.

In 1978, domestic turmoil swept the country as a result of religious and political opposition to the

Shah's rule and programs—especially SAVAK, the hated internal security and intelligence service. In January 1979, the Shah left Iran; he died abroad several years after. On February 1, 1979, exiled religious leader Ayatollah Ruhollah Khomeini returned from France to direct a revolution resulting in a new, theocratic republic guided by Islamic principles. Back in Iran after 15 years in exile in Turkey, Iraq, and France, he became Iran's national religious leader. On November 4, 1979, militant Iranian students occupied the American embassy in Tehran with the support of Ayatollah Khomeini. Fifty-two Americans were held hostage for 444 days. On April 7, 1980, the United States broke diplomatic relations with Iran, and on April 24, 1981, the Swiss Government assumed representation of U.S. interests in Tehran. Iranian interests in the United States are represented by the Pakistani Government. Following Khomeini's death on June 3, 1989, the Assembly of Experts—an elected body of senior clerics—chose the outgoing president of the republic, Ali Khamenei, to be his successor as national religious leader in what proved to be a smooth transition. In August 1989, Ali Akbar Hashemi-Rafsanjani, the speaker of the National Assembly, was elected President by an overwhelming majority. He was re-elected June 11, 1993, with a more modest majority of about 63%; some Western observers attributed the reduced voter turnout to disenchantment with the deteriorating economy.

Khomeini's revolutionary regime initiated sharp changes from the foreign policy pursued by the Shah, particularly in reversing the country's orientation toward the West. In the Middle East, Iran's only significant ally has been Syria. Iran's regional goals are dominated by wanting to establish a leadership role, curtail the presence of the U.S. and other outside powers, and build trade ties. In broad terms, Iran's "Islamic foreign policy" emphasizes: vehement anti-U.S. and anti-Israel stances; eliminating outside influence in the region; exporting the Islamic revolution; support for Muslim political movements abroad; and a great increase in diplomatic contacts with developing countries.

The Azadi Tower, Tehran

Chahar Bagh School, Isfahan

This Phrase Book contains the Persian words and expressions you are most likely to need. *All the words are written in a spelling which you read like English.* Each letter or combination of letters is used for the sound it normally represents in English and it always stands for the same sound. Thus, "oo" is always to be read as in *too, boot, tooth, roost,* never as in *blood* or *door.*

Syllables that are accented — that is, pronounced louder than others — are written in capitals.

3

Special Points

E *or* **EH**   as in *let, red, ten*. Examples: "GEL" meaning "mud," "SEH" meaning "three."

A   as in *cat, tag, man*. Examples: "BAD" meaning "bad," "NA" meaning "no."

O‿oo   is the *ow*-sound in *show, throw, slow*. Examples: "awb-JO‿oo" meaning "beer," "MO‿ooz" meaning "bananas."

Ḥ   with a dot underneath stands for an *h*-sound that comes at the end of a word or syllable. Examples: "RAWḤ" meaning "road," "moaḥ-KAM" meaning "strong."

Ḳ   with a dot underneath stands for a *k*-sound pronounced far back in the throat. Examples: "ḳay-CHEE" meaning "scissors," "SHARḲ" meaning "east."

KH   is like the sound you make when you clear your throat. Examples: "KHOOB" meaning "good," "YAKH" meaning "ice."

GH   is another sound pronounced far back in the throat, like *k* and *kh*. It is something like the sound you make in gargling. Examples: "GHARB" meaning "west," "cheh-RAWGH" meaning "a light."

J̲   when underlined, stands for the sound we have in *measure, usual, division, occasion*. Example: "j̲oo-EN" meaning "June."

4

How To Use This Phrase Book

The Table of Contents lists the situations covered. Try to become familiar with this so that you will know where to find a given section when you need it. In each section you will find a number of questions, each one so phrased that the Persian speaker will answer Yes or No, point out the direction, give you a number, etc. If you don't get an answer you can understand, use one of the following expressions:

English	Pronunciation	Persian Spelling
Answer Yes or No	HAW yaw NA ja-VAWB bed-eh-heed	ها یا نه جواب بدهید
Show me	neh-SHAWN bed-eh-heed	نشان بدهید
Write it	AWN-raw BEN-ev-ee-seed	آنرا بنویسید
Write the number	a-DAD-raw BEN-ev-ee-seed	عددرا بنویسید

The expression for "please" is "khaw-HESH mee-ko-nam":

Please show me	khaw-HESH mee-ko-nam, neh-SHAWN bed-eh-heed	خواهش میکنم نشان بدهید

You may find it helpful to point to the question in Persian and ask the Persian speaker to point to the answer:

Point to the answer in this book	ja-VAW-beh so-AWL-raw TOO-yeh een keh-TAWB neh-SHAWN bed-eh-heed	جواب سوءالرا توی این، کتاب نشان بدهید

It is a good idea to memorize the words for "Yes" and "No," the numbers (at least up to ten), and other expressions you will constantly need. You will also be able to read Persian numbers if you learn the forms of the numerals up to ten. Although some of the Persian numerals look different from ours, the system of writing numbers in Persian is the same as in English. To write twenty-three, you just put a Persian 2 followed by a Persian 3; to write four hundred sixty-eight, you first put a 4, then a 6, then an 8.

If you need a particular word, look in the Alphabetical Word List at the back of the book.

Detail, 19TH century copper tray by Abd Al-Mutallib

Fill-in Sentences

Many of the expressions are given in the form of fill-in sentences, each containing a blank which you fill in with any of the words in the list that follows. For example, if you want to know where the station is, you can look either in the section headed Location or in the one headed Roads and Transportation. You will find an expression for "Where is ____?" and, in the list following it, the words for "the railroad station." You then combine them as follows:

Where is ____?	____ ko-jawst?	ــ كجااست؟
the railroad station	eest-GAW-heh RAW-heh aw-HAN	ایستگاه راه آهن
Where is the railroad station?	eest-GAW-heh RAW-heh aw-HAN ko-jawst?	ایستگاه راه آهن کجااست؟

Sometimes the blank has to be filled in with the name of a city or a person. For example:

How far is ____?	____ az een-JAW CHEH ḳadr DOO-rast?	ــ از اینجا چقدر دور است؟
____ wants to see you	____ MEE-khaw-had sho-MAW-raw BEB-ee-nad	ــ میخواهد شمارا ببیند

7

EMERGENCY EXPRESSIONS

ASKING HELP

English	*Pronunciation*	*Persian Spelling*
Help me	MA-raw ko-MAK ko-need	مرا کمک کنید
I have lost my way	RAW-ham-raw GOAM kar-deh am	راهم را گم کرده ام
Do you understand?	MEE-fa-hmeed?	میفهمید؟
Yes	BA-leh	بله
No	NA	نه
I don't understand	NA-mee-fa-hmam	نمیفهمم
Speak slowly	ya-VAWSH HARF bez-an-eed	یواش حرف بزنید
Say it again	doab-aw-REH beg-oo-eed	دوباره بگوئید
Please	khaw-HESH mee-ko-nam	خواهش میکنم
Where is the nearest town?	naz-deek-ta-REEN SHAHR ko-jawst?	نزدیکترین شهر کجاست؟

8

English	Prounciation	Persian Spelling
Please show me	khaw-HESH mee-ko-nam, neh-SHAWN bed-eh-heed	خواهش میکنم نشان بدهید
Draw a map of it	nak-SHAY-eh AWN-raw bek-ash-eed	نقشهٔ آنرا بکشید
I am an American	man em-ree-kaw-EE HAST-am	من امریکائی هستم
How can I get there?	cheh TO‿oor mee-tav-aw-nam awn-JAW BEH-ra-sam?	چطور میتوانم آنجا برسم؟

Lion and bull motif at Persepolis

9

English	Pronunciation	Persian Spelling
Is there a train?	AW-yaw RAW-heh aw-HAN HAST?	آیا راه آهن هست ؟
Where is the station?	eest-GAWH ko-jawst?	ایستگاه کجاست ؟
Is there a bus?	AW-yaw oat-o-BOOSS HAST?	آیا اتوبوس هست؟
Where can I find the bus?	ko-JAW mee-tav-aw-nam oat-o-BOOSS pay-DAW ko-nam?	کجا میتوانم اتوبوس پیدا کنم؟
Take me there	MA-raw awn-JAW beb-a-reed	مرا آنجا ببرید
I want food	gha-ZAW mee-khaw-ham	غذا میخواهم
I want water	AWB mee-khaw-ham	آب میخواهم
Where can I find food?	ko-JAW mee-tav-aw-nam gha-ZAW pay-DAW ko-nam?	کجا میتوانم غذا پیدا کنم ؟
I've been hurt	MAN zakh-MEE sho-DEH am	من زخمی شدهام

English	Pronunciation	Persian Spelling
Take me to a doctor	MA-raw doak-TOR beb-a-reed	مرا دکتر ببرید
Bring a doctor	doak-TOR bee-aw-va-reed	دکتر بیاورید

WARNINGS

English	Pronunciation	Persian Spelling
Be careful!	dek-ḲAT ko-need!	دقت کنید
Look out!	BEP-aw-eed!	بپائید

Bas-relief of a Persian bodyguard to King Darius, Persepolis

11

The Friday Mosque, Isfahan

GENERAL EXPRESSIONS

GREETINGS

English	*Pronunciation*	*Persian Spelling*
Hello	sa-LAWM	سلام
How do you do?	sa-LAWM-moan a-LAY-koam	سلام علیکم
How are you?	HAW-leh sho-MAW cheh TO‿oo-rast?	حال شما چطوراست
Very well, thank you	tesh-ak-KOR mee-ko-nam, KHAY-lee KHOO-bast	تشکر میکنم خیلی خوباست
Thank you	tesh-ak-KOR mee-ko-nam	تشکر میکنم
I am grateful	mam-NOO-nam	ممنونم
Please	khaw-HESH mee-ko-nam	خواهش میکنم
Pardon me	BEB-akh-sheed	ببخشید
Sir	aw-ḴAW	آقا
Madam *or* Miss	khaw-NOAM	خانم

13

English	Pronunciation	Persian Spelling
English	*Pronunciation*	*Persian Spelling*
Mr. ____	aw-KAW-yeh ____	آقای____
Mrs. ____	khaw-NO-meh ____	خانم ____
My name is ____	ESS-meh man ____ ast	اسم من ____ است
What is your name?	ESS-meh sho-MAW CHEEST?	اسم شما چیست ؟
Glad to meet you	az mo-law-KAW teh sho-MAW khoash-VAK-tam	از ملاقات شما خوشوقتم
Go ahead	BEF-ar-maw-eed	بفرمائید

NOTE: This is a general expression of polite and friendly treatment. It can be used in asking a person to come in, to have a seat, to take a cigarette, to go first, to help himself.

English	Pronunciation	Persian Spelling
Come in	BEE-aw-eed TOO	بیائید تو
Sit down	BEN-esh-ee-need	بنشینید
Sit ____	____ ben-esh-ee-need	____ بنشینید
here	een-JAW	اینجا
there	awn-JAW	آنجا
Please make yourself comfortable	khaw-HESH mee-ko-nam, raw-HAT ko-need	خواهش میکنم راحت کنید

English	Pronunciation	Persian Spelling
Would you like a cigarette?	see-GAWR mayl DAW-reed?	سیگار میل دارید ؟
Do you have a match?	keb-REET DAW-reed?	کبریت دارید ؟
Are you ____?	____ hast-eed?	____ هستید ؟
hungry	go-ro-SNEH	گرسنه
thirsty	tesh-NEH	تشنه
Good-by	kho-DAW haw-FEZ	خدا حافظ
Good night	SHAB beh khayr	شب بخیر
Good morning	SOAB-heh sho-MAW beh KHAYR	صبح شما بخیر
I'll see you again	BAWZ sho-MAW-raw MEE-bee-nam	باز شمارا می بینم
I'll see you later	BAD sho-MAW-raw MEE-bee-nam	بعد شمارا می بینم
I'll see you tomorrow	far-DAW sho-MAW-raw MEE-bee-nam	فردا شمارا می بینم
I hope to see you soon	o-meed-VAW-ram beh zoo-DEE sho-MAW-raw BEB-ee-nam	امیدوارم بزودی شمارا ببینم

15

English	Pronunciation	Persian Spelling
God be with you *or* Good luck	kho-DAW beh ham-RAWH	خدا بهمراه

GETTING INFORMATION

English	Pronunciation	Persian Spelling
Yes	BA-leh	بله
No	NA	نه
Maybe	SHAW-yad	شايد
Certainly	al-bat-TEH	البته
Doubtless	bee-SHAK	بی‌شك
I don't know	NA-mee-daw-nam	نميدانم
I think so	ga-MAWN mee-ko-nam	گمان ميكنم
I don't think so	ga-MAWN NA-mee-ko-nam	گمان نميكنم
What languages do you speak?	CHEH zab-awn-HAW-ee HARF mee-za-need?	چه زبانهائی حرف ميزنيد ؟
Do you speak ___ ?	___ harf mee-za-need?	ــ حرف ميزنيد ؟
Arabic	a-ra-BEE	عربی

English	Pronunciation	Persian Spelling
French	fa-rawn-seh-VEE	فرانسوی
German	al-maw-NEE	آلمانی
Hindustani	hen-DEE	هندی
Russian	roo-SEE	روسی
Turkish	tor-KEE	ترکی
I speak ___	___ harf mee-zan-am	___ حرف میزنم
I don't speak well	KHOOB harf NA-mee-zan-am	خوب حرف نمیزنم
Can you get an interpreter?	MEE-tav-aw-need mo-tar-JEM pay-DAW ko-need?	میتوانید مترجم پیدا کنید ؟
I don't understand	NA-mee-fa-hmam	نمیفهمم
Speak slowly	ya-VAWSH harf bez-an-eed	یواش حرف بزنید
Do you understand?	MEE-fa-hmeed?	میفهمید ؟
What?	CHEH?	چه ؟
Repeat	tek-RAWR ko-need	تکرار کنید
What do you call this?	EEN-raw CHEH mee-goo-eed?	اینرا چه میگوئید؟

17

English	Pronunciation	Persian Spelling
What is this?	EEN CHEEST?	این چیست؟
What is that?	AWN CHEEST?	آن چیست؟
Wait a moment	ḴAD-ree SABR ko-need	قدری صبر کنید
Come with me	baw MAN bee-aw-eed	با من بیائید
_____ wants to see you	_____ MEE-khaw-had sho-MAW-raw BEB-ee-nad	ــ میخواهد شمارا ببیند
I want to ask you a few questions	MEE-khaw-ham chand so-AWL az sho-MAW BEP-or-sam	میخواهم چند سوٴال از شما بپرسم
Answer Yes or No	HAW yaw NA ja-VAWB bed-eh-heed	ها یا نه جواب بدهید
Show me	neh-SHAWN bed-eh-heed	نشان بدهید
Write it	AWN-raw BEN-ev-ee-seed	آنرا بنویسید
Write the number	a-DAD-raw BEN-ev-ee-seed	عددرا بنویسید

18

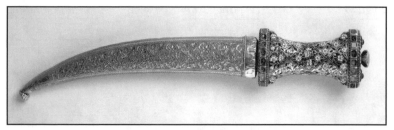

Gold dagger and sheath, 17TH century

English	Pronunciation	Persian Spelling
Point to the answer in this book	ja-VAW-beh so-AWL-raw TOO-yeh een keh-TAWB neh-SHAWN bed-eh-heed	جواب سوٴال٘را توی این کتاب نشان بدهید
Point to the number	a-DAD-raw neh-SHAWN bed-eh-heed	عددرا نشان بدهید
Draw a picture of it	AK-seh AWN-raw BEK-a-sheed	عکس آنرا بکشید

QUESTIONS ABOUT AN INDIVIDUAL

What is your nationality?	mel-lee-YA-teh sho-MAW CHEEST?	ملیت شما چیست؟

19

English	Pronunciation	Persian Spelling
Are you _____?	sho-MAW _____ hast-eed?	شما ـــ هستید؟
Arabian	a-RAB	عرب
Armenian	ar-ma-NEE	ارمنی
Assyrian	aw-shoo-REE	آشوری
French	fa-rawn-seh-VEE	فرانسوی
Indian	hen-DEE	هندی
Iranian	ee-raw-NEE	ایرانی
Kurdish	KORD	کرد
Russian	ROOSS	روس
Turkish	TORK	ترک
Are you from this region?	sho-MAW A-hleh een naw-hee-YEH hast-eed?	شما اهل این ناحیه هستید؟
Where are you from?	A-hleh ko-JAW hast-eed?	اهل کجا هستید؟
I'm from _____	A-hleh _____ hast-am	اهل ـــ هستم
Where do you live?	ko-JAW man-ZEL daw-reed?	کجا منزل دارید؟

English	Pronunciation	Persian Spelling
I live in ____	____ man-ZEL daw-ram	____ منزل دارم
Where are you going?	ko-JAW mee-ra-veed?	کجا میروید؟
I am going to ____	____ mee-ra-vam	____ میروم
Where are your friends?	ro-fa-KAW-yeh sho-MAW ko-JAW hast-and?	رفقای شما کجا هستند؟
Are they ____?	____ hast-and?	____ هستند؟
near	naz-DEEK	نزدیک
far	DOOR	دور
Where is your ____?	____ sho-MAW ko-jawst?	____ شما کجاست؟
father	peh-DA-reh	پدر
mother	maw-DA-reh	مادر

Caravansaries on old trade route

21

Palace in Tehran

English	Pronunciation	Persian Spelling
husband	sho‿oo-HA-reh	شوهر
wife	a-YAW-leh	عیال
Where is your family?	khaw-nev-aw-DAY-eh sho-MAW ko-JAW hast-and?	خانواده شما کجا هستند؟

Ark-e Ban Castle, Kermân

Wind tower, Borujerdi house, Kâshân

A Lydian, Persepolis

Vali Asr Square, Tehran

Tile panel at Isfahan, 1600 AD

Dome of Shâh Ne'mat ollâh-e-Vali, Mâhân, Kermân

Illustrated manuscript of Shah Abbas and Khan Alam, 1633 AD

29

PERSONAL NEEDS

FOOD AND DRINK

English	Pronunciation	Persian Spelling
English	*Pronunciation*	*Persian Spelling*
I am ____	____ hast-am	هستم ____
hungry	go-ro-SNEH	گرسنه
thirsty	tesh-NEH	تشنه
Where is there water?	AWB ko-JAW hast?	آب کجا هست؟
Where is there drinking water?	AW-beh khor-DAN ko-JAW hast?	آب خوردن کجا هست؟
Where is a restaurant?	rest-o-RAWN ko-jawst?	رستوران کجا است؟
I want to buy food	MEE-khaw-ham aw-zoo-ḴEH bekh-ar-am	میخواهم آذوقه بخرم
Is this good to eat? *or* Is this good to drink?	EEN khor-da-NEEST?	این خوردنی است؟
I want ____	____ mee-khaw-ham	____ میخواهم
Give me ____	____ bed-eh-heed	____ بدهید

English	Pronunciation	Persian Spelling
Bring me ___	___ bee-aw-va-reed	___ بیاورید
food	gha-ZAW	غذا
water	AWB	آب
beans	loo-bee-AW	لوبیا
beef	GOOSH-teh GAWV	گوشت گاو
beets	cho-ghoan-DAR	چغندر
bread	NAWN	نان
butter	ka-REH	کره
cabbage	ka-LAM	کلم
candy	shee-ree-NEE	شیرینی
cheese	pa-NEER	پنیر
chicken	joo-JEH	جوجه
chocolate	sho-ko-LAWT	شکلات
eggs	TOAKH-meh MORGH	تخم مرغ
fish	maw-HEE	ماهی

31

English	Pronunciation	Persian Spelling
lamb	GOOSH-teh bar-REH	گوشت بره
lentils	a-DASS	عدس
lettuce	kaw-HOO	کاهو
meat	GOOSHT	گوشت
pork	GOOSH-teh KHOOG	گوشت خوك
potatoes	seeb-za-mee-NEE	سیب زمینی
rice		
uncooked	beh-RENJ	برنج
cooked	po-LO‿oo	پلو
soup		
European style	SOOP	سوپ
Persian style thin soup with meat and vegetables	awb-GOOSHT	آبگوشت
Persian style thick soup	AWSH	آش
spinach	ess-feh-NAWJ	اسفناج
squash	ka-DOO	کدو

English	Pronunciation	Persian Spelling
tomatoes	GO‿oo-jeh fa-rang-GEE	گوجه فرنگی
turnips	shal-GHAM	شلغم
vegetables	sab-ZEE	سبزی
apples	SEEB	سیب
bananas	MO‿ooz	موز
cherries		
tart	aw-loo-baw-LOO	آلو بالو
sweet	gee-LAWSS	گیلاس
coconuts	nawr-GEEL	نارگیل
dates	khor-MAW	خرما
grapes	ang-GOOR	انگور
lemons		
tart	lee-moo-TORSH	لیمو ترش
sweet	lee-moo-shee-REEN	لیمو شیرین
mangoes	am-BEH	انبه
oranges	por-teh-ḴAWL	پرتقال
peaches	ho-LOO	هلو
pears	go-law-BEE	گلابی

English	Pronunciation	Persian Spelling
pineapples	a-na-NAWSS	ا ناس
plums	aw-LOO	آلو
strawberries	toot-fa-rang-GEE	توت فرنگی
watermelon	hen-dev-aw-NEH	هندوانه
beer	awb-JO‿oo	آ بجو
boiled water	AW-beh joo-shee-DEH	آب جوشیده
brandy	koan-YAWK	کنیاك
coffee	ka-HVEH	قهوه
cream	sar-SHEER	سرشیر
drinking water	AW-beh khor-DAN	اب خوردن
milk	SHEER	شیر
tea	chaw-EE	چای
wine	sha-RAWB	شراب
pepper	fel-FEL	فلفل
salt	na-MAK	نمك
sugar	sha-KAR	شکر

34

English	Pronunciation	Persian Spelling
vinegar	sayr-KEH	سرکه
a cup	fen-JAWN	فنجان
a fork	chang-GAWL	چنگال
a glass	gee-LAWSS	گیلاس
a knife	KAWRD	کارد
a plate	poash-ḲAWB	پشقاب
a spoon	ḳaw-SHOAḲ	قاشق
I want it ___	___ mee-khaw-ham	ــ میخواهم
cooked *or* baked	poakh-TEH	پخته
raw *or* uncooked	na-poakh-TEH	نپخته
rare	NEEM poakh-TEH	نیم پخته
well done	KHOOB poakh-TEH	خوب پخته
boiled	awb-PAZ	آب پز
broiled	bayr-YAWN	بریان
fried	sorkh-kar-DEH	سرخ کرده
roasted	beh-resh-TEH	برشته

35

LODGING

English	Pronunciation	Persian Spelling
Where is a hotel?	meh-hmawn-khaw-NEH ko-jawst?	مهمانخانه کجااست؟
I want to spend the night	MEE-khaw-ham SHAB-raw BEM-aw-nam	میخواهم شبرا بمانم
I want ____	____ mee-khaw-ham	ــــ میخواهم
a bed	TAKH-teh KHAWB	تخت خواب
bedding	RAKH-teh KHAWB	رخت خواب
blankets	pa-TOO	پتو
hot water	AW-beh GARM	آب گرم

Ornament on top of a pillar at Persepolis

36

English	Pronunciation	Persian Spelling
insecticide	da-VAW-yeh ha-sha-reh-KOASH	دوای حشره کش
the key	keh-LEED	کلید
a light	cheh-RAWGH	چراغ
mosquito netting	pash-sheh-BAND	پشه بند
a pillow	baw-LESH	بالش
a room	o-TAWḴ	اطاق
soap	saw-BOON	صابون
toilet paper	kaw-GHA-zeh ta-haw-RAT	کاغذ طهارت
a towel	ho‿oo-LEH	حوله
Where is the toilet?	mo-sta-RAWḤ ko-jawst?	مستراح کجااست؟
I want _____	MEE-khaw-ham _____	میخوهم —
to sleep	BEKH-aw-bam	بخوابم
to wash my hands and face	da-sto-ROO besh-oo-ram	دست ورو بشورم

37

English	Pronunciation	Persian Spelling
to bathe	sho-sto-SHOO ko-nam	شستشو کنم
Call me at ____ o'clock	saw-AT-eh ____ MA-raw seh-DAW ko-need	ساعت ____ مرا صدا کنید
Have you a message for me?	ba-RAW-yeh man pay-GHAW-mee DAW-reed?	برای من پیغامی دارید؟
Give this message to ____	een pay-GHAWM-raw beh ____ bed-eh-heed	این پیغامرا به ____ بدهید
Here's my address	EE-nast aw-DRESS-eh MAN	این است آدرس من
Send my mail to this address	kaw-ghaz-HAW-yeh MA-raw beh EEN aw-DRESS BEF-eh-rest-eed	کاغذهای مرا با این آدرس بفرستید
Send my things	ass-BAW-beh MA-raw BEF-eh-rest-eed	اسباب مرا بفرستید
I shall return ____	____ BAR mee-gar-dam	____ برمیگردم
tomorrow	far-DAW	فردا
Wednesday	ROO-zeh cheh-hawr-sham-BEH	روز چهارشنبه

English	Pronunciation	Persian Spelling
Have you a ____ room?	o-TAW-ḳeh ____ DAW-reed?	اطاق ــ دارید؟
better	beḥ-TA-ree	بهتری
larger	bo-zorg-TA-ree	بزرگتری
cheaper	ar-zawn-TA-ree	ارزانتری

MEDICAL AID

English	Pronunciation	Persian Spelling
Where is a ____?	____ ko-jawst?	ــ کجااست؟
Call a ____	____ seh-DAW ko-need	ــ صدا کنید
doctor	doak-TOR	دکتر
dentist	dan-dawn-SAWZ	دندانساز
ambulance	oat-o-mo-BEE-leh beḥ-daw-REE	اتومبیل بهداری
nurse	pa-ra-STAWR	پرستار
Quick!	ZOOD!	زود
Stop the bleeding	jeh-LO‿oo-eh KHOON-raw beg-ee-reed	جلو خونرا بگیرید
A tourniquet!	sha-ra-yawn-BAND!	شریان بند

English	Pronunciation	Persian Spelling
Tie it here	een-JAW beb-an-deed	اینجا ببندید
Above the wound	baw-LAW-yeh ZAKHM	بالای زخم
I am sick	MAN naw-KHOASH hast-am	من ناخوش هستم
He is sick	OO naw-KHO-shast	او ناخوش‌است
I am wounded	MAN zakh-MEE hast-am	من زخمی هستم
He is wounded	OO zakh-MEEST	او زخمی‌است
____ hurts	____ DARD mee-ko-nad	ــ درد میکند
My head	SA-ram	سرم
My tooth	dan-DAW-nam	دندانم
My back	ka-MA-ram	کمرم
My stomach	DEL-am	دلم
I am hurt here	een-JAWM sad-MEH khor-DEH	اینجام صدمه خورده
I am hurt in the ____	dar ____ sad-MEH khor-DEH am	در ــ صدمه خورده ام

40

English	Pronunciation	Persian Spelling
He is hurt in the ____	dar ____ sad-MEH khor-DEH ast	در ــــ صدمه‌خورده است
head	SAR	سر
face	soo-RAT	صورت
ear	GOOSH	گوش
eye	CHASHM	چشم
nose	da-MAWGH	دماغ
mouth	da-HAN	دهن
jaw	FAK	فك
throat	ga-LOO	گلو
neck	gar-DAN	گردن
shoulder	shaw-NEH	شانه
arm	baw-ZOO	بازو
elbow	aw-RANJ	آرنج
hand	DAST	دست
lower back	ka-MAR	کمر
upper back	POASHT	پشت

English	Pronunciation	Persian Spelling
chest	see-NEH	سینه
stomach	sheh-KAM	شکم
privates	oۯoo-ra-TAYN	عورتین
leg	SAW-ḳeh PAW	ساق پا
knee	zaw-NOO	زانو
ankle	ḳoo-ZA-keh PAW	قوزك پا
foot	PAW	پا
Bring ____	____ bee-aw-va-reed	____ بیاورید
a bandage	BAN-deh ZAKHM	بند زخم
a blanket	pa-TOO	پتو
some blankets	CHAND-taw pa-TOO	چند تا پتو
boiled water	AW-beh joo-shee-DEH	آب جوشیده
cotton	pam-BEH	پنبه
a disinfectant	da-VAW-yeh ZED-deh o-foo-NEE	دوای ضد عفونی

42

English	Pronunciation	Persian Spelling
drinking water	AW-beh khor-DAN	آب خوردن
hot water	AW-beh GARM	آب کرم
ice	YAKH	یخ
a knife	KAWRD	کارد
a sedative	da-VAW-yeh mo-sak-KEN	دوای مسکن
sheets	mal-aw-FEH	ملافه
something to tie with	yek CHEE-zee ba-RAW-yeh ba-STAN	یك چیزی برای بستن
splints	takh-TAY-eh o-sto-khawn-BAND	تخته استخوان بند
a stimulant	da-VAW-yeh mo-hay-YEJ	دوای مهیج
Do not touch ____	____ DAST NAZ-an-eed	ــ دست نزنید
Do not move ____	____ ha-ra-KAT NAD-eh-heed	ــ حرکت ندهید
Lift ____ carefully	baw dek-KAT ____ bo-LAND ko-need	با دقت ــ بلند کنید
me	MA-raw	مرا

43

English	Pronunciation	Persian Spelling
him	OO-raw	اورا
them	awn-HAW-raw	آنهارا
Be careful	dek-ḲAT ko-need	دقت كنيد
Do not give him that	AWN-raw beh OO NA-deh-heed	آنرا باو ندهيد
water	AWB	آب
food	gha-ZAW	غذا

BUYING AND PERSONAL SERVICES

Where to Get It

Where is a ____?	____ ko-jawst?	ــــ كجااست؟
barber	sal-maw-NEE	سلمانى

View of Persepolis

English	Pronunciation	Persian Spelling
bathhouse	ham-MAWM	حمام
drugstore	da-vaw-khaw-NEH	دواخانه
grocery	baḳ-ḳaw-LEE	بقالی
movie	see-na-MAW	سینما
restaurant	rest-o-RAWN	رستوران
tailor	khay-YAWT	خیاط

Things Wanted

I want to buy ____	MEE-khaw-ham ____ BEKH-a-ram	میخواهم ____ بخرم
Where can I find ____?	ko-JAW mee-tav-aw-nam ____ pay-DAW ko-nam?	کجا میتوانم ____ پیدا کنم؟
I want ____	____ mee-khaw-ham	____ میخواهم
Give me ____	____ bed-eh-heed	____ بدهید
this	EEN-raw	اینرا
that	AWN-raw	آنرا
one of these	YEK-ee az een-HAW-raw	یکی از اینهارا

English	Pronunciation	Persian Spelling
ammonia	am-o-nee-AWK	امونیاك
aspirin	aw-speh-REEN	آسپرین
a bandage	BAN-deh ZAKHM	بند زخم
batteries	baw-TREE	باطری
a belt	ka-mar-BAND	کمربند
a brush for clothes	maw-hoot-pawk-KOAN	ماهوت پاك کن
buttons	doag-MEH	دگمه
cigarettes	see-GAWR	سیگار
cloth	pawr-CHEH	پارچه
a coat	KOAT	کت
a comb	shaw-NEH	شانه
cotton	pam-BEH	پنبه
a disinfectant	da-VAW-yeh ZED-deh o-foo-NEE	دوای ضد عفونی
envelopes	paw-KAT	پاکت
a flashlight	cheh-rawgh-BAR-keh da-STEE	چراغ برق دستی

46

English	Pronunciation	Persian Spelling
foot powder	POO-dreh PAW	پودر پا
gloves	dast-KESH	دست کش
goggles	ay-NA-keh GARD-o-KHAWK	عینك گرد و خاك
handkerchiefs	dast-MAWL	دستمال
a hat	ko-LAWḤ	کلاه
ink	mo-rak-KAB	مرکب
iodine	YOAD	ید
a knife	KAWRD	کارد
a laxative	moass-HEl.	مسهل
a light bulb	LAWM-peh cheh-rawgh-BARḲ	لامپ چراغ برق
matches	keb-REET	کبریت
a needle	soo-ZAN	سوزن
an overcoat	pawl-TO	پالتو
pants	shal-VAWR	شلوار
paper	kaw-GHAZ	کاغذ

47

English	Pronunciation	Persian Spelling
a pen	ḳa-LAM	قلم
a pencil	meh-DAWD	مداد
pins	san-JAWḲ	سنجاق
quinine	gen-eh-geh-NEH	گنه‌گنه
a raincoat	baw-raw-NEE	بارانی
rubbing alcohol	al-KO-leh maw-LESH	الکل مالش
a safety razor	khoad-ta-RAWSH	خودتراش
safety razor blades	TEE-gheh khoad-ta-RAWSH	تیغ خودتراش
a scarf	SHAW-leh gar-DAN	شال گردن
scissors	ḳay-CHEE	قیچی
shaving cream	kha-MEE-reh reesh-ta-raw-SHEE	خمیر ریش تراشی
a shirt	pee-raw-HAN	پیراهن
shoelaces	BAN-deh KAFSH	بند کفش
shoes	KAFSH	کفش
soap	saw-BOON	صابون

English	Pronunciation	Persian Spelling
socks	joo-RAWB	جوراب
sunglasses	ay-NA-keh doo-DEE	عینک دودی
thread	NAKH	نخ
a toothbrush	mess-VAWK	مسواك
toothpaste	kha-MEE-reh dan-DAWN	خمیر دندان
underwear	zeer-POOSH	زیرپوش
Have you something else?	CHEE-zeh dee-GAR DAW-reed?	چیز دیکر دارید؟
More	beesh-TAR	بیشتر

Services Wanted

I want this ——	MEE-khaw-ham, EEN —— sha-vad	میخواهم این ــ شود
washed	sho-STEH	شسته
pressed	o-TOO	اتو
cleaned	ta-MEEZ	تمیز

49

English	Pronunciation	Persian Spelling
repaired	ta-MEER	تعمیر
Where can I have this ____?	ko-JAW mee-tav-aw-nam EEN-raw BED-eh-ham ____?	کجا میتوانم اینرا بدهم ــــ ؟
washed	BESH-oo-rand	بشورند
pressed	o-TOO ko-nand	اتو کنند
cleaned	ta-MEEZ ko-nand	تمیز کنند
mended	ta-MEER ko-nand	تعمیر کنند
I want to hire ____	MEE-khaw-ham ____ keh-raw-YEH ko-nam	میخواهم ــــ کرایه کنم
I want to borrow ____	MEE-khaw-ham ____ ḴARZ ko-nam	میخواهم ــــ قرض کنم
this	EEN-raw	اینرا
that	AWN-raw	آنرا
I want ____	____ mee-khaw-ham	ــــ میخواهم
a guide	raw-hna-MAW	راهنما
a porter	ham-MAWL	حمال

English	Pronunciation	Persian Spelling
a taxi	tawk-SEE	تاکسی
someone to help	yek na-far ko-MAK	یکنفر کمك
Give me a haircut	SA-ram-raw BEZ-a-need	سرمرا بزنید
Give me a shave	REE-sham-raw BET-a-raw-sheed	ریشمرا بتراشید

Payment

How much?	CHAN-dast?	چنداست؟
How much is ____?	____ CHAN-dast?	ــــ چنداست؟
This is American money	EEN POO-leh em-ree-kaw-EEST	این پول آمریکائی است
It is worth ____	____ mee-ar-zad	ــــ می ارزد
That's too much	KHAY-lee zee-AW-dast	خیلی زیاداست
I will give ____	____ mee-deh-ham	ــــ میدهم
Will you sell this for ____?	EEN-raw ____ mee-fo-roo-sheed?	اینرا ــــ میفروشید؟

English	Pronunciation	Persian Spelling
How much do I owe you?	CHAND shoad?	چند شد؟
I want a receipt	ra-SEED mee-khaw-ham	رسید میخواهم
Here is a receipt	EE-nast ra-SEED	ایناست رسید
Take it to this address	AWN-raw beh EEN aw-DRESS BEB-a-reed	آنرا باین آدرس ببرید
You will be paid on delivery	BAD az taḥ-VEEL beh sho-MAW POOL daw-DEH KHAW-had shoad	بعد از تحویل بشما پول داده خواهد شد

Jug with goddess face, 6TH century

LOCATION AND TERRAIN

LOCATION

English	*Pronunciation*	*Persian Spelling*
What place is this?	EEN-jaw KO-jawst?	اینجا کجاست؟
Show me on this map	ROO-yeh een nak SHEH neh-SHAW-nam bed-eh-heed	روی این نقشه نشانم بدهید
Have you a map?	nak-SHEH-ee DAW-reed?	نقشهای دارید؟
Can you draw me a map of it?	MEE-ta-vaw-need nak-SHAY-eh AWN-raw ba-RAW-yeh man BEK-ash-eed?	میتوانید نقشه آنرا برای من بکشید؟
Can you guide me?	MEE-tav-aw-need MA-raw raw-hnam-aw-EE ko-need?	میتوانید مرا راهنمائی کنید؟

English	Pronunciation	Persian Spelling
Can you find us a guide?	MEE-tav-aw-need yek naf-ar raw-hna MAW ba-RAW-yeh maw pay-DAW ko-need?	میتوانید یکنفر راهنما برای ما پیدا کنید؟
Where is ____?	____ ko-jawst?	____ کجااست؟
the town	SHAHR	شهر
the nearest town	naz-deek-ta-REEN SHAHR	نزدیکترین شهر
the railroad station	eest-GAW-heh RAW-heh aw-HAN	ایستگاه راه آهن
a telephone	tel-eh-FOAN	تلفن
the U. S. consulate	koan-soal-khaw-NAY-eh em-ree-KAW	کنسولخانه آمریکا
the police station	ka-lawn-ta-REE	کلانتری
Is there a ____ near here?	naz-DEE-keh een-JAW ____ HAST?	نزدیك اینجا ____ هست؟
river	rood-khaw-NEH	رودخانه
well	CHAWH	چاه

English	Pronunciation	Persian Spelling
railroad	RAW-heh aw-HAN	راه آهن
telephone exchange	mar-KA-zeh tel-eh-FOAN	مرکز تلفن
small town *or* village	DEH	ده
town or city	SHAHR	شهر
What is its name?	ESS-meh awn CHEEST?	اسم آن چیست؟
What others are there?	dee-GAR cheh hast?	دیگر چه هست؟
In which direction?	ko-DAWM ta-raf-ast?	کدام طرف است؟
Point to it	baw ang-GOASHT neh-SHAWN bed-eh-heed	با انگشت نشان بدهید
Thank you	mam-NOO-nam	ممنونم
Show me	neh-SHAWN bed-eh-heed	نشان بدهید
Which way is north?	sha-MAWL ko-DAWM ta-raf-ast?	شمال کدام طرف است؟
This way	EEN ta-RAF	این طرف
That way	AWN ta-RAF	آن طرف

55

English	Pronunciation	Persian Spelling
To the ____	ta-RA-feh ____	طرف ــــ
left	CHAP	چپ
right	RAWST	راست
north	sha-MAWL	شمال
northeast	sha-MAW-leh SHARḲ	شمال شرق
east	SHARḲ	شرق
southeast	jo-NOO-beh SHARḲ	جنوب شرق
south	jo-NOOB	جنوب
southwest	jo-NOO-beh GHARB	جنوب غرب
west	GHARB	غرب
northwest	sha-MAW-leh GHARB	شمال غرب
Here	een-JAW	اینجا
There	awn-JAW	آنجا

DISTANCE

How far is ____?	____ az een-JAW CHEH ḳadr DOO-rast?	ــــ از اینجا چقدر دوراست؟

56

English	Pronunciation	Persian Spelling
Is it _____?	_____ ast?	؟است ــ
far	DOOR	دور
very far	khay-lee DOOR	خیلی دور
near	naz-DEEK	نزدیك
One kilometer	YEK kee-lo-METR	یك كیلومتر
_____ kilometers	_____ kee-lo-METR	كیلومتر ــ
_____ meters	_____ METR	متر ــ

NOTE: For numbers 1 — 1,000, see page 71.

One mile	YEK MEEL	یك میل
_____ miles	_____ MEEL	میل ــ
How many kilometers is it from here?	az een-JAW CHAND kee-lo-MET-rast?	از اینجــا جنــد كیلومتر است؟

NOTE: A kilometer is about ⅝ of a mile. A meter is about 39 inches.

NATURE OF TERRAIN

Are you familiar with this country?	baw va-zee-YA-teh een mam-leh-KAT awsh-NAW HAST-eed?	با وضعیت این مملكت آشنا هستید؟

English	Pronunciation	Persian Spelling
Is the land ____?	za-MEE-nash ____ ast?	زمینش ــــ است؟
rocky *or* stony	sang-LAWKH	سنگلاخ
flat	SAWF	صاف
dry	KHOASHK	خشك
wet	mar-TOOB	مرطوب
muddy	gel-aw-LOOD	گل‌آلود
passable	ḳaw-BEL-eh o-BOOR	قابل عبور
Does it have ____?	____ DAW-rad?	ــــ دارد؟
glaciers	rood-khaw-NAY-eh YAKH	رودخانه یخ
hills	tap-PEH	تپه
jungles *or* woods	jang-GAL	جنگل
lakes	dar-yaw-CHEH	دریاچه
mountains	KOOḤ	کوه
passes	gar-da-NEH	گردنه
paths	jawd-DEH	جاده

English	Pronunciation	Persian Spelling
rivers	rood-khaw-NEH	رودخانه
roads	RAWḤ	راه
springs	chesh-MEH	چشمه
wells	CHAWḤ	چاه
Is the water deep?	AWB GO‿oo-dast?	آب گوداست؟
Are the mountains high?	koo-HAW bo-LAN-dand?	کوهها بلندند؟
Is the current swift	ja-ra-YAW-neh AWB TOAN-dast?	جریان آب تنداست؟
Is there a bridge?	POAL HAST?	پل هست؟

Mosque in Mashhad

ROADS AND TRANSPORTATION

ROADS AND BRIDGES

English	Pronunciation	Persian Spelling
Where does this road lead?	een RAWḤ beh ko-JAW mee-rav-ad?	اینراه به کجامیرود؟
What town does this road lead to?	een RAWḤ beh ko-DAWM shaḥr mee-rav-ad?	این راه به کدام شهر میرود؟
It leads to _____	beh _____ mee-rav-ad	به ــــ میرود
Is the road _____?	RAWḤ _____ ast?	راه ــــ است؟
Is this bridge _____?	een POAL _____ ast?	این پل ــــ است؟
good	KHOOB	خوب
bad	BAD	بد
passable	ḳaw-BEL-eh o-BOOR	قابل عبور

English	Pronunciation	Persian Spelling
Are there ____ ?	awn-JAW ____ HAST?	آنجا ــ هست؟
bridges	POAL	پل
detours	RAW-heh far-EE	راه فرعی
fords	go-zar-GAWH	گذرگاه
guideposts	a-law-MA-teh raw-hna-MAW	علامت راهنما
guides	raw-hna-MAW	راهنما
mud puddles	go‿oo-dawl-HAW-yeh gel-o-AWB	گودالهای گل و آب
obstructions	ma-vaw-NEH	موانع
narrow stretches	jawd-DAY-eh baw-REEK	جاده باریك
potholes *or* ruts	dass-san-DAWZ	دست انداز
snowdrifts	too-DAY-eh BARF	توده برف

English	Pronunciation	Persian Spelling
What is the _____?	_____ CHEEST?	_____ چیست؟
speed limit	HAD-deh ak-SA-reh sor-AT	حد اکثر سرعت
usual speed	sor-AT-eh ma-moo-LEE	سرعت معمولی
Do you know the road?	RAW-hraw MEE-daw-need?	راهرا میدانید؟
Please guide us	khaw-HESH mee-ko-nam, MAW-raw raw-hna-maw-EE ko-need	خواهش میکنم مارا راهنمائی کند
We will pay you	beh sho-MAW POOL mee-deh-heem	بشما پول میدهیم
Where can we cross the river?	rood-khaw-NEH-raw az ko-JAW mee-tav-aw-neem o-BOOR ko-neem?	رودخانه‌را از کجا میتوانیم عبور کنیم؟
How deep is the river?	go͜oo-DEE-eh rood-khaw-NEH CHEEST?	گودی رودخانه چیست؟
Is there _____ on the bottom?	TA-hash _____ DAW-rad?	تهش _____ دارد؟
mud	GEL	گل

62

English	Pronunciation	Persian Spelling
rock	SANG	سنگ
sand	SHEN	شن

RAILROADS, BUSES, PLANES

Where's the ____?	____ ko-jawst?	ــ کجااست؟
air field	fo-rood-GAWḤ	فرودگاه
bus station	eest-GAW-heh oat-o-BOOSS	ایستگاه اتوبوس
railroad station	eest-GAW-heh RAW-heh aw-HAN	ایستگاه راه آهن
baggage room	am-BAW-reh ass-BAWB	انبار اسباب
ticket office	bel-eet-for-roo-SHEE	بلیط فروشی
When does a ____ leave?	KAY ____ ha-ra-KAT mee-ko-nad?	کی ــ حرکت میکند؟
When does the ____ get here?	KAY ____ vaw-RED mee-shav-ad?	کی ــ وارد میشود؟
When does the ____ get there?	____ KAY mee-ra-sad?	ــ کی میرسد؟

English	Pronunciation	Persian Spelling
Is the ____ running?	____ KAWR mee-ko-nad?	ـــ کار میکند؟
bus	oat-o-BOOSS	اتوبوس
plane	hav-aw-pay-MAW	هواپیما
train	ka-TAWR	قطار
A ticket to ____	YEK beh-LEET beh ____	یک بلیط به ـــ
What's the fare to____?	keh-raw-YEH beh ____ CHAN-dast?	کرایه به ـــ چنداست؟
When do we get to ____?	KAY ____ mee-ra-seem?	کی ـــ میرسیم؟
Give me a timetable	YEK jad-VA-leh o-oo-KAWT bed-eh-heed	یک جدول اوقات بدهید

OTHER MEANS OF TRANSPORTATION

Where can I find ____?	ko-JAW mee-tav-aw-nam ____ pay-DAW ko-nam?	کجا میتوانم ـــ پیدا کنم؟
a bicycle	doach-ar-KHEH	دوچرخه

English	Pronunciation	Persian Spelling
a boat	ka-ra-JEE	کرجی
a camel	sho-TOR	شتر
a car	oat-o-mo-BEEL	اتومبیل
a carriage	dor-oash-KEH	درشکه
a donkey	o-LAWGH	الاغ
a horse	ASB	اسب
a mule	kaw-TAYR	قاطر
a plane	hav-aw-pay-MAW	هواپیما
a sleigh	dor-oash-KAY-eh bar-FEE	درشکه برفی
a wagon	gaw-REE	گاری

REPAIRS AND SUPPLIES

Where can I find _____?	ko-JAW mee-tav-aw-nam _____ pay-DAW ko-nam?	کجامیتوانم ــــ پیدا کنم؟
a battery	baw-TREE	باطری
brake fluid	ro‿oo-GHA-neh tor-MOAZ	روغن ترمز

65

English	Pronunciation	Persian Spelling
a cable	SEE-meh ko-LOAFT	سیم کلفت
chains	zan-JEER	زنجیر
Diesel oil	ro‿oo-GHA-neh dee-ZEL	روغن دیزل
distilled water	AW-beh mo-kat-TAR	آب مقطر
an electrician	el-ek-treek-CHEE	الکتریکچی
a garage	gaw-RAWJ	گاراژ
gasoline	ben-ZEEN	بنزین
a gas station	ben-zeen-fo-roo-SHEE	بنزین فروشی
grease	geh-REESS	گریس
an inner tube	law-STEE-keh too-EE	لاستیک تونی
a jack	JAK	جک
a light bulb	LAWM-peh cheh-RAWGH	لامپ چراغ
a mechanic	mek-aw-NEEK	مکانیک
oil	ró‿oo-GHAN	روغن
pliers	am-bor-DAST	انبر دست

English	Pronunciation	Persian Spelling
a screwdriver	aw-chawr-peech-goosh-TEE	آچار پیچ گوشتی
spark plugs	SHAM-eh oat-o-mo-BEEL	شمع اتومبیل
a tire	law-STEE-keh ROO	لاستیک رو
tire patches	va-SLAY-eh law-STEEK	وصله لاستیک
a tire pump	to-loam-BEH	تلمبه
tire tools	ab-ZAW-reh law-STEEK	ابزار لاستیک
a wrench	aw-chawr-CHARKH	آچار چرخ

Illustrated manuscript by Riza-I Abbasi 1634 AD

67

COMMUNICATIONS

RADIO AND TELEPHONING—NUMBERS

English	*Pronunciation*	*Persian Spelling*
Calling ___	haw-LO‿oo ___	هالو ___
This is ___	een-JAW ___ ast	اینجا ___ است
Answer	ja-VAWB bed-eh	جواب بده
Go ahead	BEF-ar-maw-eed	بفرمائید
Wait	SABR koan	صبر کن
Erase *or* Cancel	baw-TEL koan	باطل کن
Verify and repeat	ra-see-deh-GEE va tek-RAWR ko-need	رسیدگی و تکرار کنید
Received	ra-SEED	رسید
Acknowledge	ra-SEED goo-eed	رسید گوئید

English	Pronunciation	Persian Spelling
Repeat	tek-RAWR ko-need	تکرار کنید
Is this correct?	EEN do-RO-stast?	این درست است؟
That is correct	do-RO-stast	درست است
Can you hear me?	MA-raw MEE-sha-na-veed?	مرا میشنوید؟
I can't hear	NA-mee-sha-na-vam	نمیشنوم
That is all	ha-MEEN	همین
Urgent	fo‿oo-REE	فوری
Do not answer	ja-VAWB law-zem NEEST	جواب لازم نیست
Hello	haw-LO‿oo	هالو
Number please? (Where do you want to call?)	ko-JAW-raw mee-khaw-heed?	کجارا میخواهید؟
What is your number?	noam-RAY-eh sho-maw CHEEST?	نمره شما چیست؟

Illustrated manuscript, 1570 AD

Head of Darius, carved at Behistun

English	Pronunciation	Persian Spelling
Hang up your receiver	goo-SHEE-raw beg-o-zaw-reed	گوشی را بگذارید
The line is busy	SEEM mash-GHOO-last	سیم مشغول است
Information	et-tel-aw-AWT	اطلاعات
Supervisor	naw-ZEM-eh tel-ef-oan-khaw-NEH	ناظم تلفن خانه
They do not answer	ja-VAWB NA-mee-deh-hand	جواب نمیدهند
Here's your party	ta-RA-feh sho-MAW haw-ZEH-rast	طرف شما حاضراست
Are you through?	ta-MAWM kar-deed?	تمام کردید؟
I will ring again	BAWZ ham ZANG mee-zan-am	بازهم زنگ میزنم
There is a call for you	PAW-yeh tel-eh-FOAN sho-MAW-raw MEE-khaw-hand	پای تلفن شمـارا میخواهند
I must interrupt— I have an urgent call from ____	SEEM-raw baw-yad ḴAT ko-nam—az ____ mo-khaw-beh-RAY-eh fo‿oo-REE daw-ram	سیم را باید قطع کنم از ــــ مخابره فوری دارم

70

English	Pronunciation	Persian Spelling
Shall I ring again?	bawz ZANG bez-an-am?	باز زنگ بزنم؟
I will call you back	bawz seh-DAW-tawn mee-ko-nam	باز صداتان میکنم
What number do you want?	CHEH noam-REH-ee mee-khaw-heed?	چه نمره میخواهید؟
Give me the number of ____	noam-RAY-eh ____ bed-eh	نمره ____ بده
What is the charge?	CHEH ḳadr BAW-yad dawd	چقدر باید داد
The other party will pay the charge	POO-leh tel-eh-FOAN-raw ta-RAF mee-deh-had	پول تلفنرا طرف میدهد
Good-by	kho-DAW haw-FEZ	خداحافظ

Numbers

Numbers	Pronunciation	Persian Numerals
0	SEFR	
1	YEK	

71

Numbers	Pronunciation	Persian Numerals
2	DO	٢
3	SEH	٣
4	cheh-HAWR	٤
5	PANJ	٥
6	SHEESH	٦
7	HAFT	٧
8	HASHT	٨
9	NOḤ	٩
10	DAḤ	١٠
11	yawz-DAḤ	١١
12	dav-awz-DAḤ	١٢
13	seez-DAḤ	١٣
14	cheh-hawr-DAḤ	١٤
15	poanz-DAḤ	١٥
16	shoanz-DAḤ	١٦
17	heev-DAḤ	١٧
18	heej-DAḤ	١٨

Numbers	Pronunciation	Persian Numerals
19	nooz-DAḤ	۱۹
20	BEEST	۲۰
21	BEEST-o YEK	۲۱
22	BEEST-o DO	۲۲
30	SEE	۳۰
40	cheh-HEL	٤۰
50	pan-JAWḤ	٥۰
60	SHAST	٦۰
70	haf-TAWD	۷۰
80	hash-TAWD	۸۰
90	na-VAD	۹۰
100	SAD	۱۰۰
1,000	heh-ZAWR	۱۰۰۰

TELEGRAPH

| I want to send a ___ | MEE-khaw-ham ___ BEF-eh-rest-am | میخواهم ــ بفرستم |

English	Pronunciation	Persian Spelling
telegram *or* cablegram	tel-eg-RAWF	تلگراف
Please give me a blank form	khaw-HESH mee-ko-nam, yek FOR-mee bed-eh-heed	خواهش میکنم یك فرمی بدهید
Can I send a telegram to _____? (*name of place*)	MEE-tav-aw-nam tel-eg-RAW-fee beh _____ BEF-eh-rest-am?	میتوانم تلگرافی به ___ بفرستم؟
How much does it come to?	CHAND mee-sha-vad?	چند میشود؟
Send it collect	POO-leh tel-eg-RAWF-raw baw ta-RAF-ast	پول تلگراف بـا طرف است
Answer prepaid	ja-VAWB ka-BOO-last	جواب قبول است

MAIL

Where is the post office?	poast-khaw-NEH ko-jawst?	پستخانه کجاست؟
Where can I mail this?	ko-JAW mee-tav-aw-nam EEN-raw beh POAST bed-eh-ham?	کجا میتوانم اینرا به پست بدهم؟

74

English	Pronunciation	Persian Spelling
How much postage on this?	CHEH ḳadr TAMR law-ZEM daw-rad?	چقدر تمبر لازم‌دارد؟
Registered	sef-aw-reh-SHEE	سفارشی
Registered with return receipt	sef-aw-reh-SHEE-eh doaḳ-ab-ZEH	سفارشی دوقبضه
Insured	bee-MEH sho-DEH	بیمه شده
Value ___	ḳee-MAT ___	___ قیمت
Air mail	PO-steh hav-aw-EE	پست هوائی
What does this package contain?	moaḥ-ta-VEE-eh een bass-TEH CHEEST?	محتوی این بسته چیست؟
Books	keh-TAWB	کتاب
Candy	shee-ree-NEE	شیرینی
Clothing	leh-BAWSS	لباس
Food	khor-da-NEE	خوردنی
You may open it	MEE-tav-aw-need BAWZ ko-need	میتوانید باز کنید
Perishable	zaw-yeh-sho-da-NEE	ضایع‌شدنی
Fragile	shek-a-sta-NEE	شکستنی

75

Illustrated manuscript by Riza-I Abbasi 1634 AD

English	Pronunciation	Persian Spelling
Handle with care	baw eh-tee-YAWT ham-lo-NAKL shav-ad	با احتیاط حمل و نقل شود
Give me _____ worth of stamps	_____ TAMR bed-eh-heed	ــــ تمبر بدهید
Mail this for me	EEN-raw beh POAST bed-eh	این را به پست بده

NUMBERS, SIZE, TIME, LETTERS, ETC.

AMOUNT

English	Pronunciation	Persian Spelling
A few *or* several	CHAND-taw	چند تا
Many	zee-AWD	زیاد
Not many	NA-zee-awd	نه زیاد
Very many	KHAY-lee zee-AWD	خیلی زیاد

ORDINAL NUMBERS

NOTE: For numbers 1 — 1,000, see page 71.

First	ya-KOAM	یکم
Second	doav-VOAM	دوم
Third	sev-VOAM	سوم
Fourth	cheh-haw-ROAM	چهارم
Fifth	pan-JOAM	پنجم

English	Pronunciation	Persian Spelling
Sixth	shee-SHOAM	ششم
Seventh	haf-TOAM	هفتم
Eighth	hash-TOAM	هشتم
Ninth	no-HOAM	نهم
Tenth	da-HOAM	دهم
Eleventh	yawz-da-HOAM	يازدهم
Twelfth	dav-awz-da-HOAM	دوازدهم

SIZE AND WEIGHT

English	Pronunciation	Persian Spelling
Small	koo-CHEK	كوچك
Large	bo-ZORG	بزرك
Medium	mee-aw-NEH	ميانه
Long	deh-RAWZ	دراز
Short *or* low	koo-TAWḤ	كوتاز
High	bo-LAND	بلند
Heavy	sang-GEEN	سنگين
Light	sa-BOAK	سبك

English	Pronunciation	Persian Spelling
English	*Pronunciation*	*Persian Spelling*

TIME

NOTE: For numbers, see page 71.

English	Pronunciation	Persian Spelling
What time is it?	saw-AT CHAN-dast?	ساعت چنداست؟
It's five o'clock	saw-AT-eh PAN-jast	ساعت پنجاست
It's ten minutes past five	saw-AT-eh PAN-jo DAH da-kee-ḲEH ast	ساعت پنجو ده دقیقه است
It's half past five	saw-AT-eh PAN-jo NEE-mast	ساعت پنجو نیماست
Ten minutes to six	saw-AT-eh SHEESH DAH da-kee-ḲEH KAM	ساعت شش ده دقیقه کم
Today	em-ROOZ	امروز
Yesterday	dee-ROOZ	دیروز
Tomorrow	far-DAW	فردا
In the morning	SOAB	صبح
In the afternoon	BAD az ZOAḤR	بعد از ظهر
In the evening	av-VA-leh SHAB	اول شب

79

English	Pronunciation	Persian Spelling
At sunrise	to-LOO-eh awf-TAWB	طلوع آفتاب
At dusk	gho-ROOB	غروب
At noon	ZOAHR	ظهر
At midnight	NESS-feh SHAB	نصف شب
At night	SHAB	شب
Sunday	yek-sham-BEH	یکشنبه
Monday	doash-am-BEH	دوشنبه
Tuesday	sesh-am-BEH	سه شنبه
Wednesday	cheh-hawr-sham-BEH	چهارشنبه
Thursday	panj-sham-BEH	پنج شنبه
Friday	joam-EH	جمعه
Saturday	sham-BEH	شنبه
January	jawn-vee-EH	ژانویه
February	fev-ree-EH	فوریه
March	MAWRSS	مارس
April	awv-REEL	آوریل

English	Pronunciation	Persian Spelling
May	MEH	مه
June	joo-EN	ژوئن
July	joo-YEH	ژوئيه
August	OOT	اوت
September	sep-TAWMBR	سپتامبر
October	oak-TOABR	اکتبر
November	no-VAWMBR	نوامبر
December	deh-SAWMBR	دسامبر
Day	ROOZ	روز
Week	haf-TEH	هفته
Month	MAWH	ماه
One day	YEK ROOZ	يك روز
Two days	DO ROOZ	دو روز
One week	YEK haf-TEH	يك هفته
Two weeks	DO haf-TEH	دو هفته
One month	YEK MAWH	يك ماه
Two months	DO MAWH	دو ماه

Persian Months

NOTE: The names of the months given in the preceding section are taken from the European calendar. These names are used by some Persians who live in the large cities or do business with European firms. But most Persians use their own calendar, which is divided into four seasons of three months each. Their New Year's Day comes on the first day of spring. The names of the Persian months and the approximate corresponding dates in our calendar are given below.

March 21 — April 21	far-var-DEEN	فروردین
April 21 — May 22	or-dee-beh-HESHT	اردیبهشت
May 22 — June 22	khor-DAWD	خرداد
June 22 — July 23	TEER	تیر
July 23 — August 23	mor-DAWD	مرداد
August 23 — September 23	sha-hree-VAR	شهریور
September 23 — October 23	MEHR	مهر
October 23 — November 22	aw-BAWN	آبان
November 22 — December 22	aw-ZAR	آذر
December 22 — January 21	DAY	دی
January 21 — February 20	ba-HMAN	بهمن
February 20 — March 21	ess-FAND	اسفند

NAMES OF THE LETTERS

Letter	Name as Pronounced	Letter	Name as Pronounced
ا	a-LEF	ص	SAWD
ب	BEH	ض	ZAWD
پ	PEH	ط	TAW
ت	TEH	ظ	ZAW
ث	SEH	ع	AYN
ج	JEEM	غ	GHAYN
چ	CHEH	ف	FEH
ح	HEH	ق	ḲAWF
خ	KHEH	ك	KAWF
د	DAWL	گ	GAWF
ذ	ZAWL	ل	LAWM
ر	REH	م	MEEM
ز	ZEH	ن	NOON
ژ	JEH	و	VAWV
س	SEEN	ه	HEH
ش	SHEEN	ی	YEH

WEIGHTS AND MEASURES

Persian System

Pronunciation	Persian Spelling	U.S. Equivalent (Approximate)	
khar-VAWR	خروار	650	pounds
MA-neh SHAWḤ	من شاه	13	pounds
MAN *or* MA-neh tab-REEZ	من تبریز	6.5	pounds
chaw-RAK	چارك	1.7	pounds

Gold throne with rubies, tourmalines, and pearls, 16TH century

Pronunciation	Persian Spelling	U.S. Equivalent (Approximate)
SEER	سیر	0.17 pound
mess-ḲAWL	مثقال	0.17 ounce
far-SANG or far-SAKH	فرسخ	3.8 miles
ZAR	ذرع	41 inches
ḳa-DAM	قدم	20 inches
geh-REH	گره	2.5 inches

Metric System

kee-lo-GRAWM or kee-LO	کیلو	2.2 pounds
hekt-o-GRAWM	هکتوگرام	3.5 ounces
geh-RAWM	گرام	0.035 ounce
kee-lo-METR	کیلومتر	0.62 mile
METR	متر	1.1 yards
sawn-tee-METR	سانتیمتر	0.39 inch

85

Bronze head of a Parthian noble, Malamir

Vaulted octagonal entrance of Chahar Bagh School, Isfahan

Pronunciation	Persian Spelling	U.S. Equivalent (Approximate)
mee-lee-METR	ميليمتر	0.039 inch
hekt-o-LEETR	هكتوليتر	26.5 gallons
LEETR	ليتر	1.06 quarts

Table of Equivalents

1 ree-AWL	=	100 dee-NAWR
1 khar-VAWR	=	100 MAN
1 MA-neh SHAWḤ	=	2 MAN
1 MAN	=	4 chaw-RAK
1 chaw-RAK	=	10 SEER
1 SEER	=	16 mess-ḲAWL
1 far-SANG	=	6,000 ZAR
1 ZAR	=	16 geh-REH
1 ḳa-DAM	=	8 geh-REH
1 kee-lo-GRAWM	=	10 hekt-o-GRAWM

1 kee-lo-GRAWM	=	1,000 geh-RAWM
1 kee-lo-METR	=	1,000 METR
1 METR	=	100 sawn-tee-METR
1 METR	=	1,000 mee-lee-METR
1 hekt-o-LEETR	=	100 LEETR

Table of Approximate Conversions

Inches to centimeters:	Multiply by 10 and divide by 4.
Yards to meters:	Multiply by 9 and divide by 10.
Miles to kilometers:	Multiply by 8 and divide by 5.
Gallons to liters:	Multiply by 4 and subtract 1/5 of number of gallons.
Pounds to kilograms:	Multiply by 5 and divide by 11.

Copper casket by Sadiq, 17TH century

IMPORTANT SIGNS

English	Persian Spelling
STOP (Traffic signal)	توقف
STOP (Road sign)	ایست
SLOW	آهسته
GO SLOW	آهسته حرکت کنید
KEEP TO THE RIGHT	از دست راست حرکت کنید
NO PARKING	توقف ممنوع است
NO ADMITTANCE	دخول ممنوع است
WOMEN	زنانه
MEN	مردانه
NO SMOKING	دخانیات ممنوع است
ENTRANCE	دخول

English	Persian Spelling
EXIT	خروج
CAUTION	احتیاط کنید
DANGER	خطر
STATION	ایستگاه
TRAFFIC PROHIBITED IN THIS DIRECTION	عبور ممنوع ابت

Main court, Chahan Bagh School, Isfahan

INTERNATIONAL ROAD SIGNS

DANGER

DANGER

MAIN ROAD AHEAD

CAUTION

SHARP TURN

RIGHT CURVE

LEFT CURVE

TAKE EITHER ROUTE

CROSSROAD

THIS WAY

DO NOT ENTER

FIRST-AID STATION

GUARDED RAIL-ROAD CROSSING **UNGUARDED RAIL-ROAD CROSSING** **NO WAITING**

NO PARKING **PARKING** **NO VEHICLES**

NO MOTOR VEHICLES **WEIGHT LIMIT 5½ TONS**

NO ANIMAL-DRAWN TRAFFIC **SPEED LIMIT** **OPEN CULVERT (DIP)**

91

ALPHABETICAL
WORD LIST

In Persian the form of a word sometimes changes according to the type of sentence in which it is used. For example, the simple form of the word for "soldier" is "sar-BAWZ." This form is used in sentences like "I am a soldier" and "Are there soldiers near here?" However, in different kinds of sentences, other forms of the word are used. In the sentence "We are American soldiers" you find the form "sar-BAW-zeh," and in the sentence "Where are American soldiers?" you find the form "sar-bawz-HAW-yeh." In this list the simple form of the word is given: "soldier" is listed as "sar-BAWZ."

A

English	*Pronunciation*
accelerator	peh-DAW-leh ben-ZEEN
address	aw-DRESS

English	Pronunciation
afternoon	**BAD** az ZOAHR
air field	fo-rood-GAWH
airplane	hav-aw-pay-MAW
alcohol, rubbing	al-KO-leh maw-LESH
altitude	ayr-teh-FAW
ambulance	oat-o-mo-BEE-leh beh-daw-REE
ammonia	am-o-nee-AWK
ankle	koo-ZA-keh PAW
answer	ja-VAWB
antenna	awn-TEN
apples	SEEB
April	awv-REEL
arm	baw-ZOO
aspirin	aw-speh-REEN
August	OOT

B

back *(of person)*,	ka-MAR
bad	**BAD**

English	Pronunciation
baggage room	am-BAW-reh ass-BAWB
bananas	MO⌣ooz
bandage	BAN-deh ZAKHM
barber	sal-maw-NEE
bathhouse	ham-MAWM
beans	loo-bee-AW
bed	TAKH-teh KHAWB
bedding	RAKH-teh KHAWB
beef	GOOSH-teh GAWV
beer	awb-JO⌣oo
beets	cho-ghoan-DAR
belt	ka-mar-BAND
better	beh-TAR
bicycle	doach-ar-KHEH
black	see-AWH
blades, safety razor	TEE-gheh khoad-ta-RAWSH
blanket	pa-TOO
blouse	bo-LOOZ

English	Pronunciation
blue	aw-BEE
boat	ka-ra-JEE
boiled	awb-PAZ
boiled water	AW-beh joo-shee-DEH
book	keh-TAWB
bottom	TAH
brake fluid	ro‿oo-GHA-neh tor-MOAZ
brakes	tor-MOAZ
brandy	koan-YAWK
bread	NAWN
bridge	POAL
bridge *(of ship)*	ar-SHAY-eh koo-CHEK-eh kash-TEE
bridle	af-SAWR
brown	ka-hveh-EE
brush *(for clothes)*	maw-hoot-pawk-KOAN
bus	oat-o-BOOSS

English		Pronunciation
bus station		eest-GAW-heh oat-o-BOOSS
butter		ka-REH
button		doag-MEH
bulb, light		LAWM-peh cheh-rawgh-BARK
	or	LAWM-peh cheh-RAWGH

C

cabbage	ka-LAM
cable	SEE-meh ko-LOAFT
cablegram	tel-eg-RAWF
camel	sho-TOR
camp	or-doo-GAWH
candy	shee-ree-NEE
car	oat-o-mo-BEEL
carriage	dor-oash-KEH
ceiling	SAKF
certainly	al-bat-TEH
chain	zan-JEER

English	Pronunciation
cherries	
(sweet)	gee-LAWSS
(tart)	aw-loo-baw-LOO
cheese	pa-NEER
chest	see-NEH
chicken	joo-JEH
chief	ra-EESS
chocolate	sho-ko-LAWT
cigarette	see-GAWR
city	SHAḤR
clerk	moan-SHEE
cloth	pawr-CHEH
clothing	leh-BAWSS
clutch	ka-LAWCH
coal	zo-ghawl-SANG
Coast Guard	pawss-DAW-reh saw-heh-LEE
coat	KOAT
coconuts	nawr-GEEL
coffee	ḳa-HVEH
color	RANG
comb	shaw-NEH

St. Stephen's Church, Jolfa

Bâgh-e Erâm Palace, Shiraz

English	Pronunciation
company	go-roo-HAWN
cook	awsh-PAZ
cooked	poakh-TEH
correct	do-ROST
cotton	pam-BEH
cream	sar-SHEER
cruiser	razm-NAWV
cup	fen-JAWN
current *(river)*	ja-ra-YAW-neh AWB

D

dates	khor-MAW
day	ROOZ
December	deh-SAWMBR
deck	ar-SHAY-eh kash-TEE
deep	GO‿ood
dentist	dan-dawn-SAWZ
detour	RAW-heh far-EE
Diesel oil	ro‿oo-GHA-neh dee-ZEL
direction	ta-RAF

English	Pronunciation
disinfectant	da-VAW-yeh ZED-deh o-foo-NEE
distilled water	AW-beh mo-ḳat-TAR
doctor	doak-TOR
donkey	o-LAWGH
doubtless	bee-SHAK
drinking water	AW-beh khor-DAN
driver	sho-FAYR
drugstore	da-vaw-khaw-NEH
dry	KHOASHK
dump	makh-ZA-neh mo-hem-MAWT
dusk	gho-ROOB

E

ear	GOOSH
east	SHARḲ
eggs	TOAKH-meh MORGH
elbow	aw-RANJ

English	Pronunciation
electrician	el-ek-treek-CHEE
engine	mo-TOR
equipment	saw-zo-BARG
evening	av-VA-leh SHAB
extinguisher, fire	aw-tesh-khaw-moosh-KOAN
eye	CHASHM

F

face	soo-RAT
family	khaw-nev-aw-DEH
far	DOOR
father	peh-DAR
February	fev-ree-EH
few	CHAND-taw
firewood	hee-ZOAM
first-aid-packet	bass-TAY-eh lav-aw-zeh-MAW-teh teb-BEE
fish	maw-HEE
flag	bay-RAK
flagship	kash-TEE-eh far-mawh-DEH-heh NAWV

English	Pronunciation
flashlight	cheh-rawgh-BAR-ķeh da-STEE
flat	SAWF
food	gha-ZAW
foot	PAW
foot powder	POO-dreh PAW
ford	go-zar-GAWḤ
fork	chang-GAWL
form, blank *(for telegram)*	FORM
fragile	shek-a-sta-NEE
Friday	joam-EH
fried	sorkh-kar-DEH
friends	ro-fa-ĶAW

G

garage	gaw-RAWJ
gas	GAWZ
gasoline	ben-ZEEN
gas station	ben-zeen-fo-roo-SHEE
glass	gee-LAWSS

English	Pronunciation
gloves	dast-KESH
good	KHOOB
Good-by	kho-DAW haw-FEZ
grapes	ang-GOOR
gravel	sang-gree-ZEH
gray	khaw-kess-tah-REE
grease	geh-REESS
green	SABZ
grocery	baḳ-ḳaw-LEE
guide	raw-hna-MAW
guidepost	a-law-MA-teh raw-hna-MAW
gun	TOOP

H

hammer	cha-KOASH
hand	DAST
handkerchief	dast-MAWL
hangar	awsh-yaw-NEH
hat	ko-LAWḤ

English	Pronunciation
head	SAR
heavy	sang-GEEN
Hello	
(greeting)	sa-LAWM
(telephone)	haw-LO‿oo
here	een-JAW
high	bo-LAND
hill	tap-PEH
horn	BOOK̟
horse	ASḂ
horseshoe	NAL
hotel	meh-hmawn-khaw-NEH
hot water	AW-beh GARM
hour	saw-AT
how	cheh TO‿oor
hungry	go-ro-SNEH
hurt	az-YAT or sad-MEH

English	Pronunciation
husband	sho‿oo-HAR

I

ice	YAKH
information *(telephone)*	et-tel-aw-AWT
ink	mo-rak-KAB
insecticide	da-VAW-yeh ha-sha-reh-KOASH
instruments	aw-LAWT
interpreter	mo-tar-JEM
iodine	YOAD
iron sheet iron	 aw-HA-neh va-RAK

J

jack	JAK
January	jawn-vee-EH
jaw	FAK
July	joo-YEH

English	Pronunciation
June	joo-EN
jungle	jang-GAL

K

key	keh-LEED
khaki	khaw-kee-RANG
kilometer	kee-lo-METR
knee	zaw-NOO
knife	KAWRD

L

ladder	nar-deh-BAWN
lake	dar-yaw-CHEH
lamb	GOOSH-teh bar-REH
language	za-BAWN
large	bo-ZORG
larger	bo-zorg-TAR
laxative	moass-HEL
left	CHAP
leg	SAW-keh PAW

105

English		Pronunciation
lemons		
(sweet)		lee-moo-shee-REEN
(tart)		lee-moo-TORSH
lentils		a-DASS
lettuce		kaw-HOO
light		cheh-RAWGH
light (weight)		sa-BOAK
light bulb		LAWM-peh cheh-rawgh-BARK
	or	LAWM-peh cheh-RAWGH
load		BAWR
long		deh-RAWZ
low		koo-TAWH
lumber		takh-TEH

M

Madam	khaw-NOAM
mangoes	am-BEH

English	Pronunciation
many	zee-AWD
map	nak-SHEH
March	MAWRSS
match	keb-REET
May	MEH
maybe	SHAW-yad
meat	GOOSHT
mechanic	mek-aw-NEEK
medium	mee-aw-NEH
message	pay-GHAWM
or	mo-khaw-beh-REH
message center	mar-KA-zeh mo-khaw-beh-RAWT
messenger	amr-BAR
meter	METR
midnight	NESS-feh SHAB
mile	MEEL
milk	SHEER
Miss	khaw-NOAM
Monday	doash-am-BEH

English		Pronunciation
money		POOL
month		MAWḤ
more		beesh-TAR
morning		SOAB
mother		maw-DAR
motor		mo-TOR
motorcycle		mo-to-see-KLET
mountain		KOOḤ
mouth		da-HAN
movie		see-na-MAW
Mr.		aw-ḳAW-yeh
Mrs.		khaw-NO-meh
mud		GEL
muddy		gel-aw-LOOD
	or	gel-LEE
mud puddles		go‿oo-dawl-HAW-yeh gel-o-AWB
mule		ḳaw-TAYR

N

nail		MEEKH
name		ESSM

English	Pronunciation
nationality	mel-lee-YAT
near	naz-DEEK
nearest	naz-deek-ta-REEN
neck	gar-DAN
needle	soo-ZAN
night	SHAB
no	NA
noon	ZOAHR
north	sha-MAWL
northeast	sha-MAW-leh SHARK
northwest	sha-MAW-leh GHARB
nose	da-MAWGH
November	no-VAWMBR
number	noam-REH
figure	a-DAD
nurse	pa-ra-STAWR

O

observer	deed-BAWN
obstructions	mav-aw-NEH

English	Pronunciation
octane rating	da-ra-JAY-eh oak-TAWN
October	oak-TOABR
oil	ro‿oo-GHAN
Diesel oil	ro‿oo-GHA-neh dee-ZEL
engine oil	ro‿oo-GHA-neh maw-SHEEN
oil viscosity	ghel-ZA-teh ro‿oo-GHAN
operator,	
radio operator	rawd-yo-CHEE
switchboard operator	tel-ef-oan-CHEE
orange (color)	naw-ran-JEE
oranges	por-teh-ḲAWL
Ordnance Department	ed-aw-RAY-eh tass-lee-HAWT
outfit	vaw-HED
overcoat	pawl-TO

P

package	bass-TEH
pants	shal-VAWR

English	Pronunciation
paper	kaw-GHAZ
pass	gar-da-NEH
passable	ḳaw-BEL-eh o-BOOR
path	jawd-DEH
patrol	gash-TEE
peaches	ho-LOO
pears	go-law-BEE
pen	ḳa-LAM
pencil	meh-DAWD
pepper	fel-FEL
perishable	zaw-yeh-sho-da-NEE
pick	ko-LANG
pigeon	kab-oo-TAR
pillow	baw-LESH
pilot	kha-leh-BAWN
pin	san-JAWḲ
pineapples	a-na-NAWSS
pistol	tap-awn-CHEH
plane	hav-aw-pay-MAW

Persian clay vessel, 6TH century

Persian Warrior, 5TH century BC

English	Pronunciation
English	*Pronunciation*
plate	poash-ḲAWB
please	khaw-HESH mee-ko-nam
pliers	am-bor-DAST
plums	aw-LOO
police station	ka-lawn-ta-REE
pork	GOOSH-teh KHOOG
porter	ham-MAWL
post office	poast-khaw-NEH
potatoes	seeb-za-mee-NEE
pothole	dass-san-DAWZ
powder, foot,	POO-dreh PAW
power plant,	kawr-khaw-NAY-eh cheh-rawgh-BARḲ
private	sar-BAWZ
propeller	par-REH
purple	ar-ghav-aw-NEE

Q

English	Pronunciation
question	so-AWL
quick	ZOOD
quinine	gen-eh-geh-NEH

English	Pronunciation
	R
radio equipment	saw-zo-BAR-geh rawd-YO
radio operator	rawd-yo-CHEE
radio repairman	rawd-yo-SAWZ
radio set	dast-GAW-heh rawd-YO
radio station	eest-GAW-heh rawd-YO
railroad	RAW-heh aw-HAN
railroad station	eest-GAW-heh RAW-heh aw-HAN
raincoat	baw-raw-NEE
raw	na-poakh-TEH
razor, safety	khoad-ta-RAWSH
razor blades	TEE-gheh khoad-ta-RAWSH
receipt,	ra-SEED
or	ḲABZ
receiver *(telephone)*	goǫ-SHEE
red	ḳayr-MEZ

English	Pronunciation
reflector	mo-na-KESS ko-nan NOOR-DAY-eh
region	naw-hee-YEH
repairs	ta-MEER
restaurant	rest-o-RAWN
rice *(cooked)*	po-LO‿oo
(uncooked)	beh-RENJ
right	RAWST
river	rood-khaw-NEH
road	RAWḤ

S

English	Pronunciation
saddle	ZEEN
salt	na-MAK
sand	SHEN
Saturday	sham-BEH
scarf	SHAW-leh gar-DAN
scissors	kay-CHEE
screwdriver	aw-chawr-peech-goosh-TEE
sedative	da-VAW-yeh mo-sak-KEN
September	sep-TAWMBR
several	CHAND-taw

114

English		Pronunciation
shaving cream		kha-MEE-reh reesh-ta-raw-SHEE
shoelaces		BAN-deh KAFSH
shoes		KAFSH
short		koo-TAWḤ
shoulder		shaw-NEH
shovel		BEEL
Sir		aw-ḲAW
sleigh		dor-oash-KAY-eh bar-FEE
slow *or* slowly		ya-VAWSH
small		koo-CHEK
snowdrift		too-DAY-eh BARF
soap		saw-BOON
socks		joo-RAWB
soup		SOOP
	or	awb-GOOSHT
	or	AWSH
south		jo-NOOB
southeast		jo-NOO-beh SHARḲ
southwest		jo-NOO-beh GHARB

115

English	Pronunciation
spark plugs	SHAM-eh oat-o-mo-BEEL
specialty	ta-khass-SOASS
speed limit	HAD-deh ak-SA-reh sor-AT
spinach	ess-feh-NAWJ
spoon	ḳaw-SHOAḲ
spring *(of water)*	chesh-MEH
squash	ka-DOO
stable	ta-vee-LEH
stamp	TAMR
station	eest-GAWḤ
bus station	eest-GAW-heh oat-o-BOOSS
railroad station	eest-GAW-heh RAW-heh aw-HAN
stimulant	da-VAW-yeh mo-hay-YEJ
stomach	sheh-KAM
stony	sang-LAWKH
strawberries	toot-fa-rang-GEE
sugar	sha-KAR

English	Pronunciation
Sunday	yek-sham-BEH
sunglasses	ay-NA-keh doo-DEE

T

tail	DOAM
tailor	khay-YAWT
tan	ZARD
taxi	tawk-SEE
tea	chaw-EE
telegram	tel-eg-RAWF
telephone	tel-eh-FOAN
telephone exchange	mar-KA-zeh tel-eh-FOAN
telephone line	SEE-meh tel-eh-FOAN
telephone receiver	goo-SHEE
tent	chaw-DOR
Thank you	tesh-ak-KOR mee-ko-nam
	or mam-NOO-nam

English		Pronunciation
there		awn-JAW
thirsty		tesh-NEH
thread		NAKH
throat		ga-LOO
Thursday		panj-sham-BEH
ticket		beh-LEET
timetable		jad-VA-leh o‿oo-KAWT
tire		law-STEE-keh ROO
	or	law-STEEK
tire patch		va-SLAY-eh law-STEEK
tire pump		to-loam-BEH
tire tools		ab-ZAW-reh law-STEEK
today		em-ROOZ
toilet		mo-sta-RAWH
toilet paper		kaw-GHA-zeh ta-haw-RAT
tomatoes		GO‿oo-jeh fa-rang-GEE
tomorrow		far-DAW

English	Pronunciation
tooth	dan-DAWN
toothbrush	mess-VAWK
toothpaste	kha-MEE-reh dan-DAWN
tooth powder	GAR-deh dan-DAWN
towel	ho‿oo-LEH
town	SHAHR
train	RAW-heh aw-HAN *or* ka-TAWR
truck	oat-o-mo-BEE-leh baw-REE
truth	RAWST
tube, inner	law-STEE-keh too-EE
Tuesday	sesh-am-BEH
turnips	shal-GHAM

U

underwear	zeer-POOSH
urgent	fo‿oo-REE
U. S. consulate	koan-soal-khaw-NAY-eh em-ree-KAW

English	Pronunciation
U. S. Government	do‿oo-LA-teh em-ree-KAW

V

value	ķee-MAT
vegetables	sab-ZEE
very	KHAY-lee
village	DEH
vinegar	sayr-KEH
visibility	pa-dee-daw-REE

W

wagon	gaw-REE
water	AWB
watermelon	hen-dev-aw-NEH
Wednesday	cheh-hawr-sham-BEH
week	haf-TEH
well *(for water)*	CHAWH

English	Pronunciation
west	GHARB
white	sa-FEED
wife	a-YAWL
wind velocity	sor-AT-eh BAWD
wine	sha-RAWB
wings	BAWL
wire	SEEM
electric wire,	SEE-meh el-ek-TREEK
wire cutters	seem-BOR
wood	jang-GAL
wound	ZAKHM
wrench	aw-chawr-CHARKH

Y

year	SAWL
yellow	ZARD
yes	BA-leh
yesterday	dee-ROOZ

Mausoleum of Hâfez, Shiraz